W9-BVM-974

GAMES ON THE MOVE!

Lisa Regan

QEB Publishing

Editor: Sarah Eason
Designer: Calcium
Illustrators: Owen Rimington and Emma DeBanks

Published in the United States by
QEB Publishing, Inc.
3 Wrigley, Suite A
Irvine, CA 92618

www.qed-publishing.co.uk

A CIP record for this book is available from the Library of Congress

ISBN 978 1 59566 933 9

Printed in China

Have fun with the games in this book, but NEVER distract the driver of the car when you play them.

CONTENTS

How to Use This Book	4
No Peeking!	6
Big Fat Zero!	7
I Spy	8
Scary Starey	9
Travel Bingo	10
Don't Laugh!	11
Fashion Fix	12
Funny Face	13
Monster Madness	14
Scribbles	15
Rock, Paper, Scissors	16
Snap!	17
Going Shopping	18
Land, Water, Air	19
Time for a Rhyme	20
Sing Along	21
Poetry, Please	22
Licensed to Spell	23
A to Z	24
A to Z Again!	25
The Name Game	26
Three Blind Sheep	27
Famous Names	28
Pyramid	29
Nine Square	30
Odds and Evens	32

HOW TO USE THIS BOOK

Welcome, come on in, hello!
Do you need a game when you're on the go?

Long journeys can be boring. It doesn't matter if you're stuck in a car or traveling by train or plane, once the first excitement wears off, you need something to pass the time. Flick through the pages of this book to find something to make the miles fly by. Here's what you'll find...

You will need

Most of the games are so easy you can just read the instructions and start playing. All you need is yourself—your eyes, ears and, mostly your brain. There are just a few games that need pencils and paper or a deck of cards. One game needs some preparation—read the instructions on page 10 (Travel Bingo) before you leave home.

Players

Chances are you're traveling with at least one other person, and most of these games are even more fun if you can persuade someone else to play too. Don't ask the person driving your car to play difficult games. It can be dangerous to drive and play at the same time. If no one else wants to play, read the "On Your Own?" section to see how to adapt the game to play quietly by yourself.

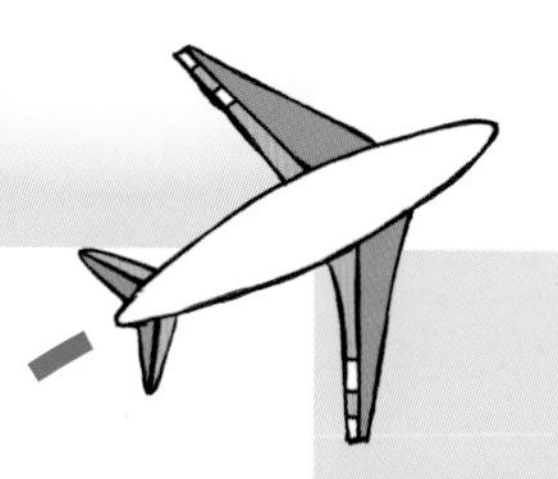

Difficulty

Travel games are supposed to be fast, simple and fun, so all of the games are pretty easy. Some of them need better writing or math skills, or a little practice before you get really good at playing. The easiest games are marked with * and are at the beginning of the book. The hardest games are at the end, marked * * * * *, and the games in between are—well, in between!

I SPY

You will need:
- your eyes and brain

I spy, with my little eye,
Lots of things as we pass by.

Difficulty: ★ Players: 2 or more

1 One player has to choose an object they can see, ideally something that won't whoosh past in the next few seconds or minutes.

2 That player says, "I spy with my little eye, something that is... blue." The other people playing take turns guessing what is being thought of, naming blue things they can see around them.

3 Let's imagine the answer is the seat they are sitting on. The player who finally guesses it then takes a turn to choose something they can see.

Bet You Can't!
Choose an object to spy that begins with a certain letter, so "something beginning with...T" could be a train or a truck.

On Your Own?
Play with passing items to spot pairs, such as two yellow cars or two things that rhyme.

The winner is...
no one—this game is played just to pass the time.

8

SCARY STAREY

You will need:
- your eyes

No matter what they say or do
Don't let the others get to you.

Difficulty: ★ Players: 2 or more

1 One player volunteers to go first. They have to stare at a fixed point—maybe the headrest in front, or a sticker on the window.

2 The other players have to try to distract him. They can make faces, make noises (but don't disturb the driver), tell jokes—anything!

3 The staring person must ignore all this, and not laugh or take his eyes off the chosen spot.

The winner is...
whoever lasts the longest.

Did You Know?
Don't try to play this game against a chameleon—its eyes can look in two different directions at once, so it would easily win.

On Your Own?
Try to stare at your chosen spot without blinking. Count the seconds to see how long you can last.

9

Bet You Can't!

Are you too good already? Bored after just one turn? Then read this section for an extra challenging twist to add. Ha, smarty-pants! Not so smart now! (Or are you?)

Did You Know?

For some games you will find fascinating facts related to them, to add to the fun.

NO PEEPING!

This game makes the time fly by,
It's so easy—give it a try!

> **You will need:**
> - just your eyes and brain

Difficulty:  **Players:** 1 or more

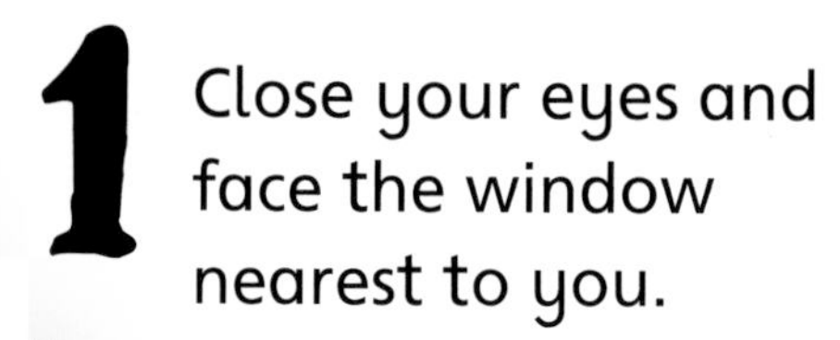

1 Close your eyes and face the window nearest to you.

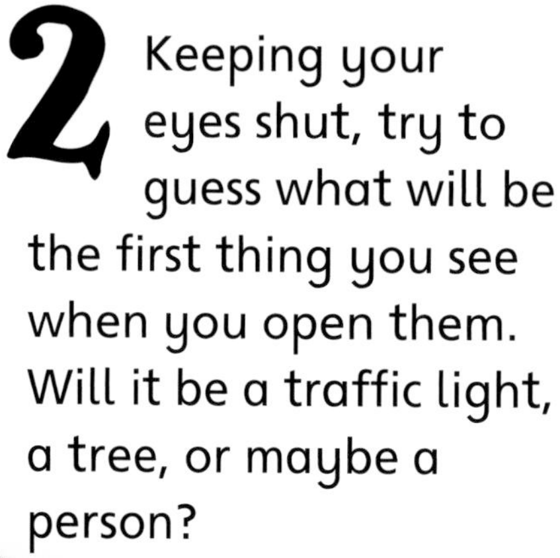

2 Keeping your eyes shut, try to guess what will be the first thing you see when you open them. Will it be a traffic light, a tree, or maybe a person?

3 Score a point if you open your eyes and your guess was right. If more than one person is playing, the other players can act as referees to make sure you don't cheat.

The winner is... the first person to score five points.

On Your Own?
You can play by yourself and see how good at guessing you are. Don't cheat!

Bet You Can't!
Can you guess the color of the first thing you'll see!

BIG FAT ZERO!

You will need:

- pencil
- paper

The aim of the game is to be a hero: Count as high as you can before dropping to zero.

Difficulty:  **Players:** any number

1 Choose something you think you'll see a lot of, such as a white car or a railroad crossing.

2 Count as many of your items as you can and keep the score on your paper—BUT there's a catch! You must also choose another thing that you won't see often—maybe a conductor or the "fasten seatbelts" sign. Every time you see it, your score goes back to zero.

3 See how high you can get before your score gets zeroed.

The winner is... the person with the highest score for the trip.

On Your Own? You can easily play this game by yourself.

Bet You Can't! Add a twist by letting another player choose your "big fat zero" item.

I SPY

You will need:

- your eyes and brain

I spy, with my little eye,
Lots of things as we pass by.

Difficulty:  **Players:** 2 or more

1 One player has to choose an object they can see, ideally something that won't whoosh past in the next few seconds or minutes.

2 That player says, "I spy with my little eye, something that is... blue." The other people playing take turns guessing what is being thought of, naming blue things they can see around them.

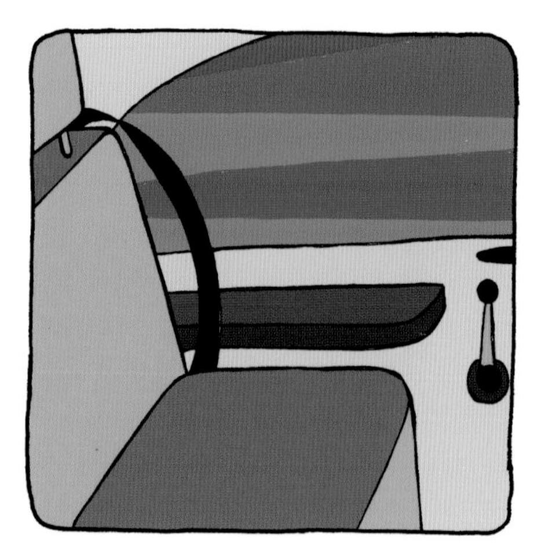

3 Let's imagine the answer is the seat they are sitting on. The player who finally guesses it then takes a turn to choose something they can see.

Bet You Can't!

Choose an object to spy that begins with a certain letter, so "something beginning with...T" could be a train or a truck.

On Your Own?

Play with passing items to spot pairs, such as two yellow cars or two things that rhyme.

The winner is...

no one—this game is played just to pass the time.

SCARY STAREY

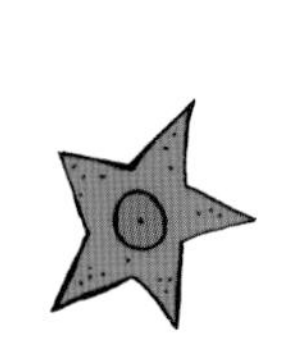

**No matter what they say or do
Don't let the others get to you.**

Difficulty: ★ **Players:** 2 or more

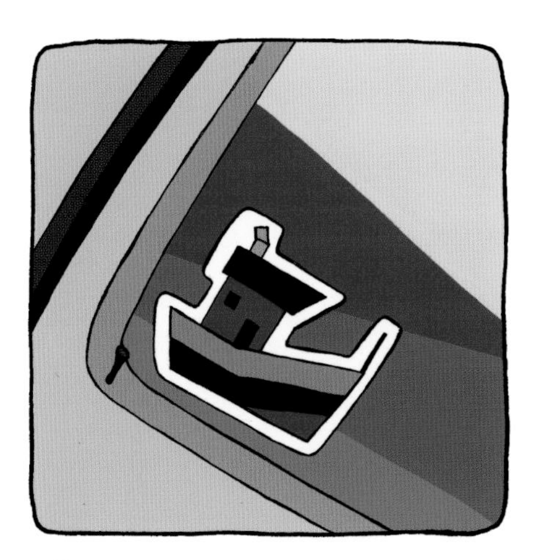

1 One player volunteers to go first. They have to stare at a fixed point—maybe the headrest in front, or a sticker on the window.

2 The other players have to try to distract him. They can make faces, make noises (but don't disturb the driver), tell jokes—anything!

3 The staring person must ignore all this, and not laugh or take his eyes off the chosen spot.

The winner is... whoever lasts the longest.

Did You Know?

Don't try to play this game against a chameleon—its eyes can look in two different directions at once, so it would easily win.

On Your Own?

Try to stare at your chosen spot without blinking. Count the seconds to see how long you can last.

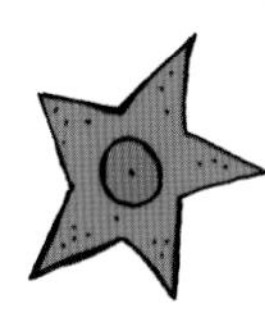

TRAVEL BINGO

Prepare this game before you play,
To help to speed you on your way.

Difficulty:  **Players:** 1 or more

You will need:
- scissors
- magazines
- paper
- glue
- pens

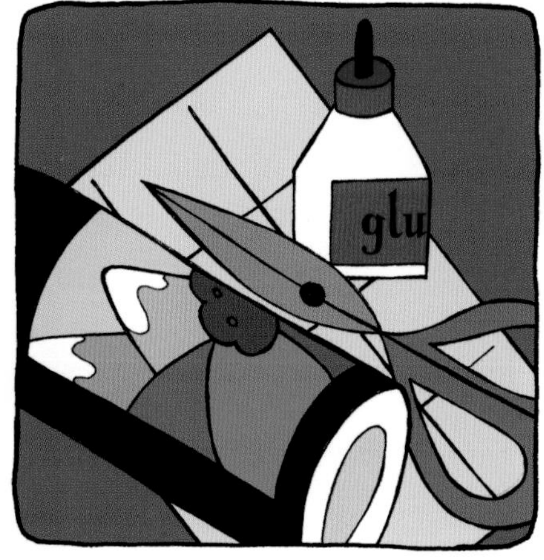

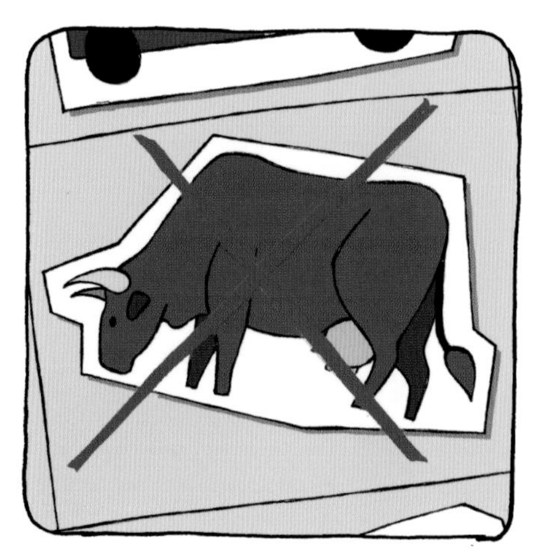

1 Prepare this game before your trip. Divide pieces of paper into nine or 12 squares. Cut pictures out of magazines and glue one in each square. Choose things you might see on your journey, such as a cow, a streetlight, or a person in uniform.

2 On the journey, give each player a "bingo card" full of pictures. When they spot an object on their card, they cross it out.

3 If you like, play so that each player can only look out of their side of the vehicle.

The winner is... the player who crosses off all of their items first.

On Your Own?

Make yourself a big bingo card with lots of items to keep you occupied for ages!

DON'T LAUGH!

You will need:

- just your face

Can your face show joy or pain?
Ask those around you on the train!

Difficulty:  **Players:** 2 or more

1 This game is best with an adult or older child acting as "caller." The caller must name an emotion—a feeling that people have.

3 The trick of the game is that you have to act out the emotion without laughing. If you laugh, you're instantly OUT!

2 The other players have to show that emotion on their faces. It might be angry, sad, surprised, hopeful—can you act those out?

The winner is...
the last person left when everyone else is out for laughing too much.

On Your Own?

Use these to get you started: frightened, disgusted, happy, in love, grumpy, fierce, nervous, bored, tired, hurt, terrified, worried–bet you're laughing by now!

Bet You Can't!

Play with sound effects. The more noises you make, the funnier it becomes.

FASHION FIX

**Check out the clothes that people choose,
Can you find flowers, or purple shoes?**

Difficulty: ★ **Players:** 2 or more

1 Each player takes turns describing an item of clothing they can see. It can be as ordinary or as unusual as you like—for example brown boots, a flowery shirt, or a yellow coat.

2 The other players look carefully at everyone around them, to see who is wearing that item.

3 Score a point for spotting it first. If no one has spotted the item after five minutes, the person who chose the clothing wins the point.

The winner is...
the player with the most points, but the real fun is finding and describing the clothes people wear!

On Your Own?
Choose a common item of clothing and count how many different people are wearing it.

Bet You Can't!
Think of random items of clothing rather than items someone can see. Everyone tries to spot the item first.

FUNNY FACE

You will need:

- just your face

To play this game you can't be shy.
It's good fun, too—go on, try!

Difficulty:  **Players:** 2 or more

1 The first player starts by saying, "I went on vacation and I made a face like this—" then makes a funny face, such as blowing out their cheeks.

2 The next player says the same thing, but besides blowing out their cheeks, they add another funny face, such as crossing their eyes.

3 The next player adds another funny face, such as sticking out their tongue. Keep playing until someone gets it wrong.

On Your Own?

You can play exactly the same game if you don't mind looking really silly!

The winner is...

the first player to forget what to do, or do it in the wrong order or whose face just won't make those awful expressions!

MONSTER MADNESS

You will need:
- pencils
- paper

Draw some monsters if you dare...
Unfold your page and see what's there.

Difficulty: ★★ **Players:** 2 or more

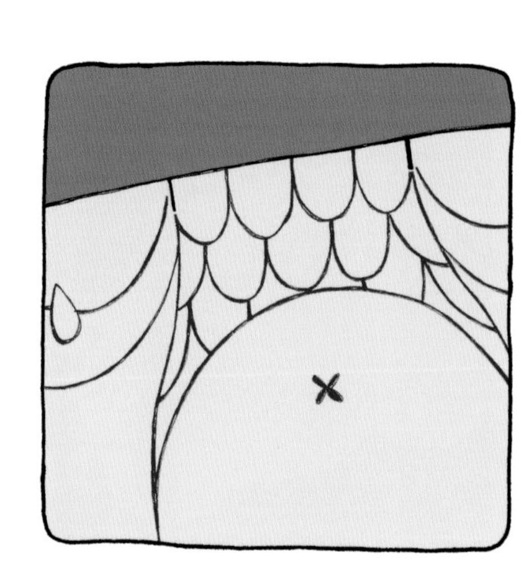

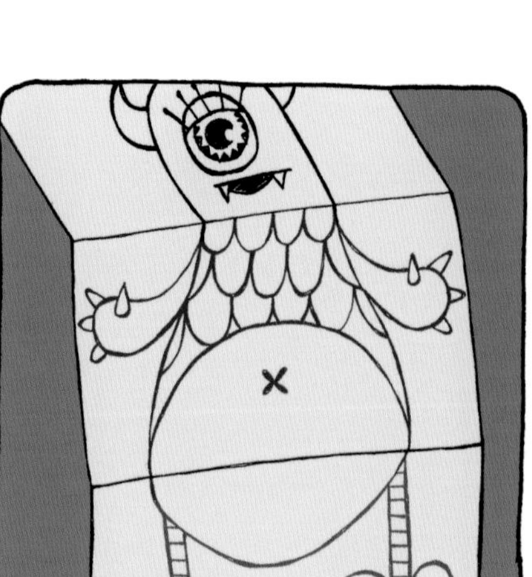

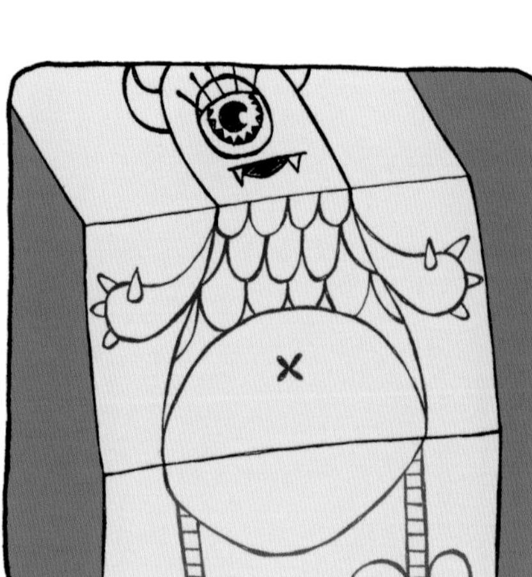

1 Each player needs a piece of paper. Draw a monster's head at the top of the page and fold down just enough paper to leave the neck showing.

2 Switch papers with another player and add a monster's body to their drawing. Don't peek under the fold.

3 Keep folding and switching to add legs, feet and a name. You can draw the scariest or the silliest body parts you can think of.

On Your Own?
You could draw the head of a friend, the body of a superhero and the feet of an animal to make yourself chuckle!

The winner is...
no one, but you could decide which monster is the silliest!

SCRIBBLES

You will need:
- felt-tip pens
- paper

Loop the loop and swirl around,
See what pictures can be found.

Difficulty: **Players:** 1 or more

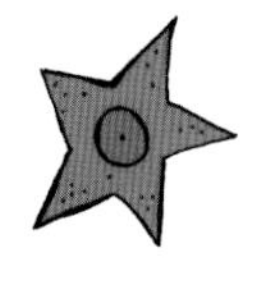

1 On a piece of paper, ask an adult or another player to draw a scribble with lots of loops and twirls.

2 Now study the scribble and see if you can either turn it into a picture of something, or color all the spaces to make a colorful design.

3 If there's more than one player, you can draw a scribble for someone else to color in. The scribbling is half the fun!

The winner is... no one—this game is just for fun.

Bet You Can't!

Instead of a scribble, ask for a pattern of about 20 dots and join them up into any shape you see in them.

On Your Own?

It's easy to draw your own scribble and then color the spaces. Try doing the scribble with your eyes closed!

ROCK, PAPER, SCISSORS

Cut it, blunt it, wrap it—hey,
It all makes sense when you start to play.

Difficulty: ★★ **Players:** 2 or 3

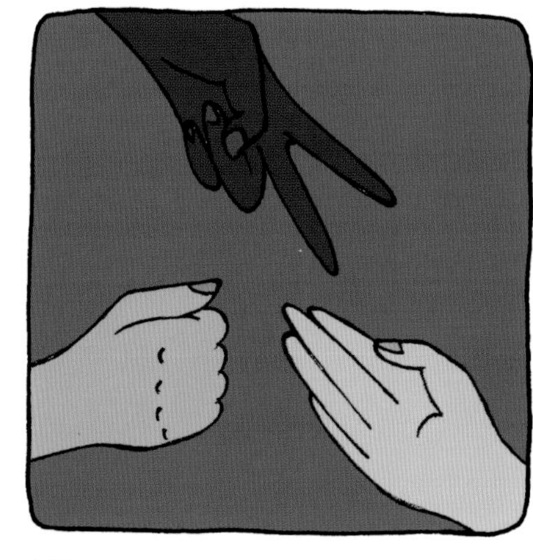

1 Everyone makes a fist, then bangs it three times on a surface. Count to three as you bang your fist, and then choose either rock, paper, or scissors.

2 For rock, keep your fist clenched. For paper, open your hand out flat. For scissors, reveal your first two fingers.

3 Your choices decide the winner: rock blunts scissors (stone wins), scissors cut paper (scissors wins), paper wraps rock (paper wins). If both of you choose the same item, it's a draw.

The winner is... usually the player who wins two out of three times—but just keep playing until you forget the score.

On Your Own?

Think of other sets of three things that could work as a game like this. Maybe penguin slides on ice, ice freezes shark, shark eats penguin?

SNAP!

You don't need cards to play this game—
Just look for things that are the same.

Difficulty:  **Players:** 2

1 Each player chooses something they can see. It's best to pick something that is not seen everywhere, but also isn't one of a kind—maybe an oil tanker, or a limousine.

2 You then have to spot another one of that thing.

3 When you see your target object, shout, "Snap!" and claim a point. Both of you can then choose a new thing.

The winner is...
the first person to get 10 points.

On Your Own?
Choose an item from a magazine and see how long it takes you to spot it around you.

Did You Know?

Don't play Snap with a crocodile—their jaws can clamp shut with more than 10 times the power of a great white shark's jaws.

GOING SHOPPING

You will need:

- pencils
- paper

**You might think that shopping's a bore,
But it's fun when you keep score!**

Difficulty:  **Players:** 2 or more

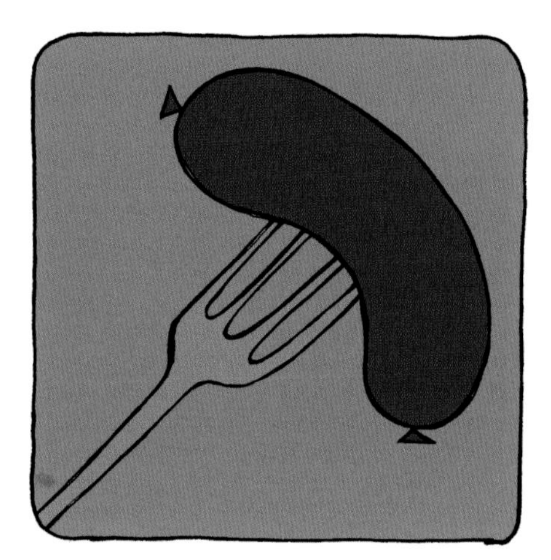

The winner is... the person who checks off all their items first.

1 Each player writes a "shopping list" of ten things, including some more difficult items—a racing car, a new party dress—and some ordinary things, like hot dogs or pencils.

2 Exchange lists with another player and then play. The idea is to check off each item as you pass a shop where you could buy it. Supermarkets don't count—you need a car showroom, clothes shop, butcher shop, or whatever.

On Your Own?
Make your own list before you start out, and play in the same way.

Did You Know?

The Mall of America in Bloomington, Minnesota is a giant mall with more than 500 shops. This game would be easy to play there!

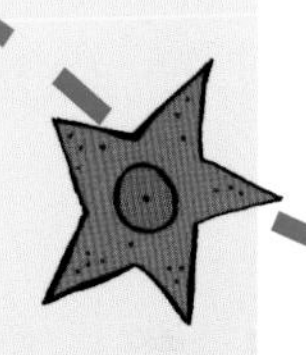

LAND, WATER, AIR

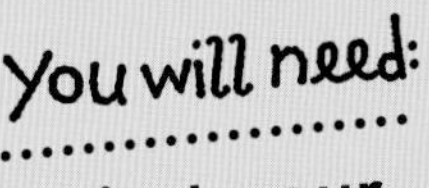

You will need:

- just your brain

Flying, swimming, crawling slow,
How many animals do you know?

Difficulty: ★★★ **Players:** any number

1 One person calls out either "land," "water," or "air."

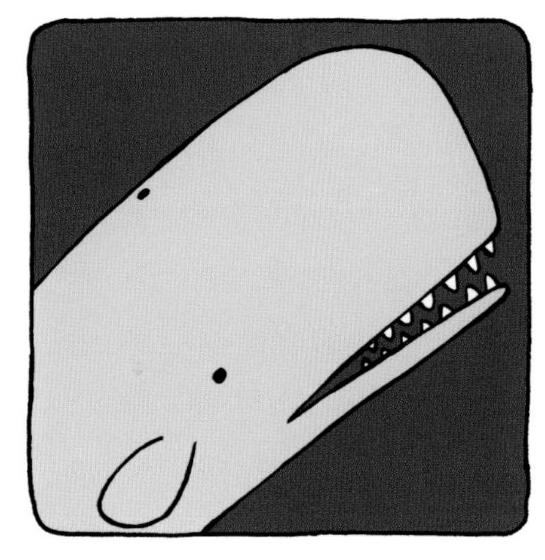

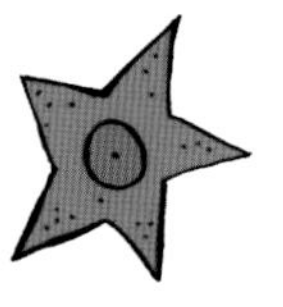

2 The other players take turns naming animals that lives in that place. For land you could say elephant, lizard or ostrich. For water you might choose whale, jellyfish or penguin. For air, bat, fly, or eagle would be correct.

3 Keep switching so that everyone gets a turn calling the places and naming the animals. You score a point for every correct answer.

The winner is... the first person to score 20 points.

On Your Own?

Write land, air, and water on pieces of paper and turn them face down. Shuffle them around and turn them over one at a time to test yourself.

TIME FOR A RHYME

You will need:

- just your brain

Counting games can pass the time,
Are you smart enough to make them rhyme?

Difficulty: ★★★ **Players:** any number

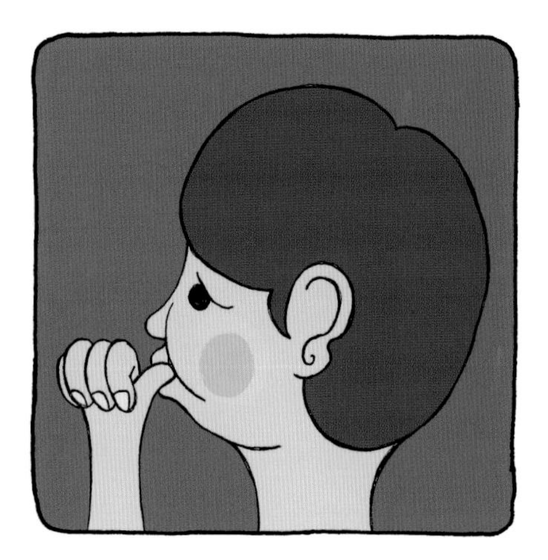

1 Start by saying, "When I was one, I..." and then add something that rhymes, such as "sucked my thumb" or "learned to run."

2 Each player takes a turn in this game—you decide whethe each turn is a new number, or if every player has their turn at number one, then two, then three and so on.

3 Keep playing, finding different rhymes for all the numbers.

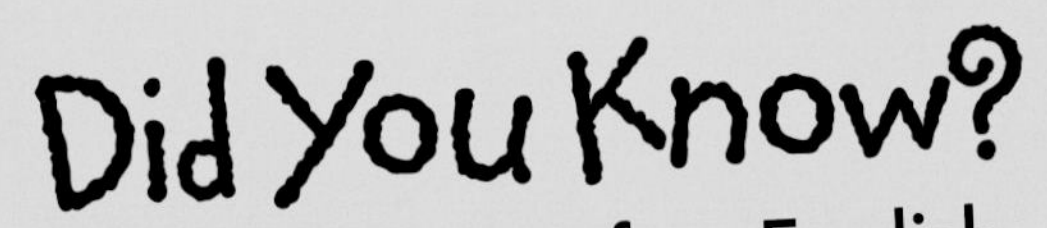

The winner is...
no one—it's just for fun.

Did You Know?

There are very few English words that rhyme with "seven." Try "oven," "heaven," or "cavern" if you're stuck.

On Your Own?

You can easily play this game on your own. See how far you can get.

SING ALONG

You will need:

- radio or MP3 player to play alone

Music makes the miles fly past,
So sing along and travel fast!

Difficulty: ☆☆☆ **Players:** any number

1 Take it in turns to be the "hummer." The hummer hums part of a well-known tune. It could be a pop song, a nursery rhyme, or the theme from a TV show.

2 The other players have to guess what the tune is.

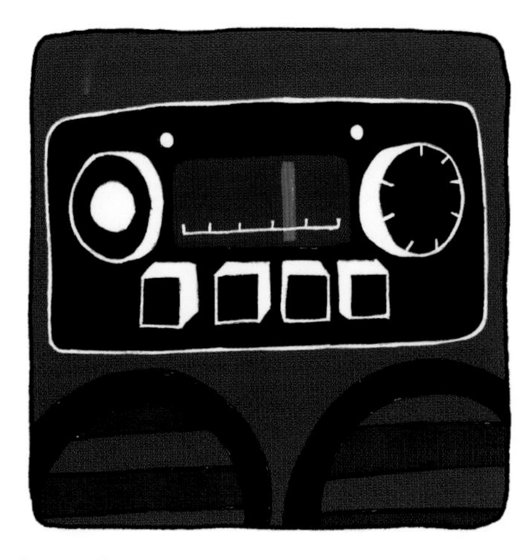

3 You can also play the "On your own" version with more than one player.

On Your Own?

Listen to songs on the radio or MP3 player and try to guess the name of the song from just the intro (the music that plays before anyone starts singing).

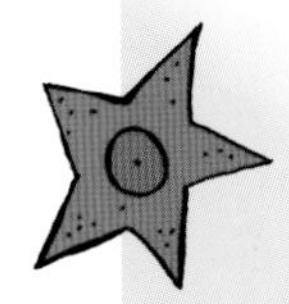

Bet You Can't!

Play without music, just by saying some words from the middle of a song. So "here I go again" is from ABBA's "Mamma Mia," and "we'll keep on fighting to the end" is from "We Are The Champions," by Queen.

The winner is...

the player who guesses the most songs.

POETRY, PLEASE!

Anyone can make a rhyme—
But can you think of one in time?

Difficulty: ★★★ **Players:** 2 or more

1 One player says a simple word, such as 'boy' or 'flower'.

2 All the other players then take turns saying a word that rhymes with it. Score a point for each word, but lose a point if you repeat another person's word.

3 When you've run out of rhymes, another person thinks of a new starting word. The words get sillier as you go along...

The winner is... the first person to score 50 points.

On Your Own?

Think up words that rhyme with something you can see. You could make up a small poem for each one.

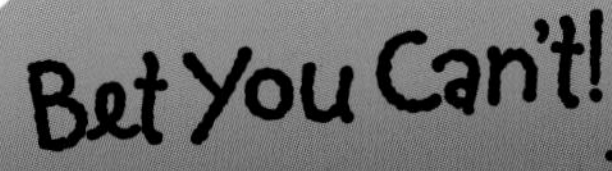

Score an extra point for every letter in a word that's longer than six letters.

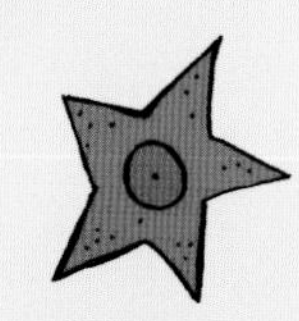

LICENSED TO SPELL

Look for Bs, and Gs, and As,
Then make up a funny phrase!

Difficulty: ★★★★ **Players:** any number

You will need:
- a pencil and paper will help

1 If you're in a car, look at the letters on the license plate of a passing vehicle. Let's imagine they are EWW. On a plane or train, (or if most of the lisence places in your state are all numbers) think of three-letter words, such as "and" or "pin."

2 Try to make up a funny sentence containing three words that begin with the letters. For this one, you could have "Every William Wins."

3 The first player to think of the sentence scores a point. Keep playing until you run out of sentences.

Bet You Can't!
Choose two licence plates and make up a six-word sentence!

The winner is...
the person who thinks of the most three-word sentences.

On Your Own?
It's easy to play this game on your own—but no cheating!

A TO Z

See which of your friends is better At spotting items for each letter.

Difficulty: ★★★★ **Players:** any number

1 Write all the letters of the alphabet, in order, on a piece of paper.

2 Look around to find something beginning with each letter. It's easy enough to find a light or a window, but can you find something beginning with Z, or X? Hmm, tricky...

3 Cross out each letter as you find something, and score a point for each letter.

The winner is... the player with the most points. You could score two points if you're the only person to spot something for a particular letter.

On Your Own?
This game is lots of fun, even on your own.

A TO Z AGAIN!

Now you REALLY need your eyes
For all the letters you must spy.

Difficulty: ★★★★ **Players:** any number

1 This game is very similar to the last one, but with a twist. Again, write down all the letters of the alphabet.

2 You are looking for an item for each letter, but you must actually SEE the letter written down—on a sign, or an ad, for example.

3 You must find at A before you can look for B. Only one player can claim each answer, so if someone spots a P for parking the other players must find P in a different place.

The winner is...
the first person to cross off all their letters.

On Your Own?
This game is great to play on your own.

Did You Know?

The letters a, b, c, and d are not used to spell any of the numbers from 1 to 99. C isn't used in any English number at all!

THE NAME GAME

You will need:

- pencil and paper to play alone

Is your name Sam, or Sue, or Spike? Be as silly as you like!

Difficulty: ★★★★ **Players:** any number

1 The first player starts with A and says, "My name is _______ and I'm _______." They have to choose a name and a describing word beginning with A, so they might say, "My name is Andrew and I'm amazing."

2 The next player uses B for their name and description: "My name is Belinda and I'm just beautiful."

3 Keep going through the alphabet, but you are only allowed 20 seconds to think of the answer each time. If you take longer, you are out of the game!

The winner is... the last person still in the game.

On Your Own?

It's easy to play this game on your own.

Bet You Can't!

Add a last name and a second describing word: "My name is Richard Rattlesnake and I'm rotten and ridiculous."

THREE BLIND SHEEP

You will need:

- just your brain

Make the words up as you go:
It could be you who steals the show.

Difficulty: ★★★★ **Players:** any number

1 The aim of this game is to make people laugh, but be careful not to disturb the car's driver.

2 One person starts singing a well-known song or rhyme. Players take turns singing a word or a line, but they can change a word to make people laugh.

3 You might end up with something like this: "Three blind sheep, three blind sheep, see how they bark, see how they bark, they all danced after the mayor's wife, who knitted their tails with a stick... " It sounds crazy but it gets everyone giggling!

On Your Own?
You can easily make up your own silly songs.

The winner is...
of course there's no winner in this game—it's too silly for that!

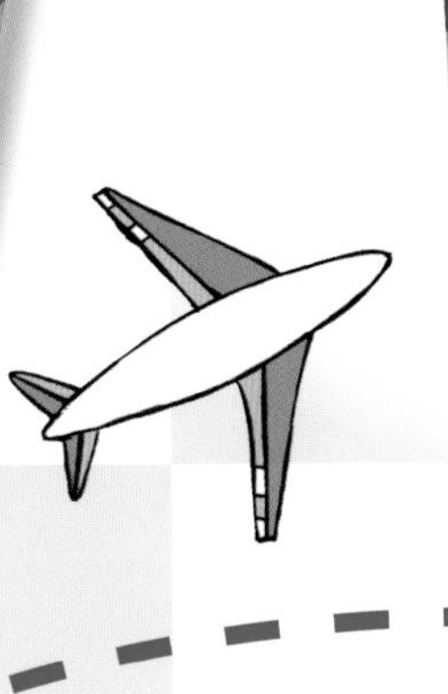

FAMOUS NAMES

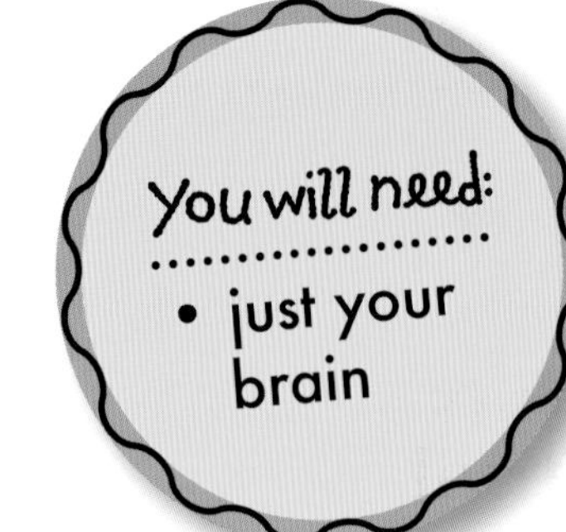

Think of people from TV:
Their names will help you win—you'll see!

Difficulty: ☆☆☆☆ **Players:** 2 or more

1 Each player names a famous person whose name begins with A—such as Angelina Jolie. They could be a pop star, sports personality, actor...anyone well-known!

2 You can set your own rules—only first names or only last names can be allowed.

3 Work your way through the alphabet. Make sure you take turns going first. It's no fun if you're always the fourth player to try to think of a name when the other players have said all the names you know.

Bet You Can't!

Change the subject to animals, sports teams, or countries.

The winner is...

anyone who makes it through the alphabet without having to pass a turn.

On Your Own?

Try thinking only of people with a single name, such as Madonna, or who have the same two initials, such as Mickey Mouse.

PYRAMID

Here's a game for on your own,
It will help to speed you home.

Difficulty: ★★★★★ **Players:** 1

1 Place one card, face up, to make the top point of a pyramid. Place two cards below it. Place a row of three below those, and a final row of four cards. Each row must slightly overlap the row above it.

2 The goal is to find pairs that add up to 13. Kings are 13, Queens are 12, Jacks are 11, and Aces are 1. You must start by taking one card from the bottom of the pyramid, and work up.

3 Take out any pairs of 13 (if there are any showing), then turn over the top card from the main pile. If you can now make 13, remove the pair. Keep turning over the cards and taking out pairs.

On Your Own?
This game is only good for one player!

The winner is...
you, if you can remove every card in the pyramid before you have turned over all the cards in the main pack.

NINE SQUARE

Another game to play with one.
Soon your journey will be done!

Difficulty: ☆☆☆☆☆ **Players:** 1 or 2

1 Divide the deck so that each player has half the cards (26 cards).

2 The first player puts down a card, face up. The second player places another card next to it. The first player then places another card, making a row of three.

3 The cards are laid out in three rows of three, making a square of nine, giving the game its name. BUT if a player puts down a card that is the same as another one already at the table, they can then cover both the matching cards with two new cards.

Did You Know?

Card games to play on your own are often called Solitaire. There are hundreds of them, and it's easy to get hooked!

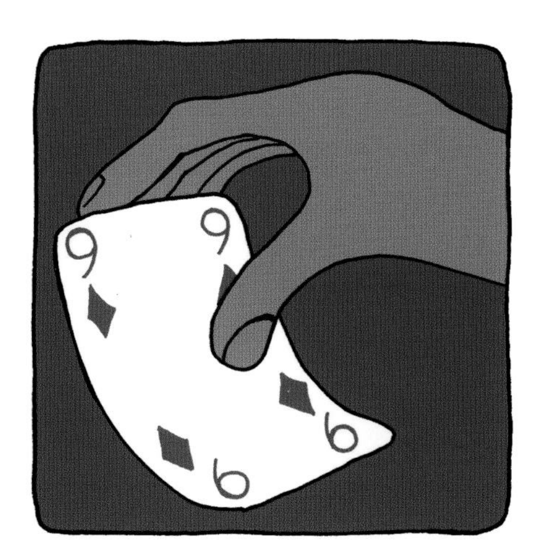

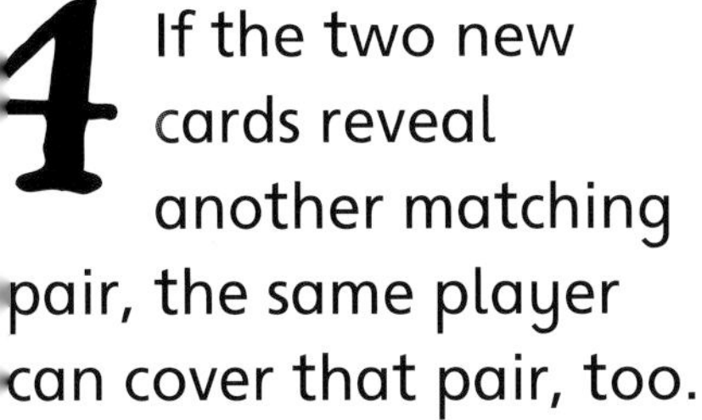

4 If the two new cards reveal another matching pair, the same player can cover that pair, too.

5 A player's turn ends when there are no more pairs to cover up. The next player puts a new card onto a new space.

6 You can add an extra rule if you're feeling brainy. Instead of covering up pairs of Jacks, Queens, or Kings, you can wait until one of each (a Jack, a Queen, and a King) shows and cover all three. It's up to you.

On Your Own?

This game was designed to play alone—just hold all the cards yourself and keep playing them onto spaces or to cover up pairs.

The winner is...

the first person to put down all their cards. Or the loser is the person who has to play the ninth unmatched card.

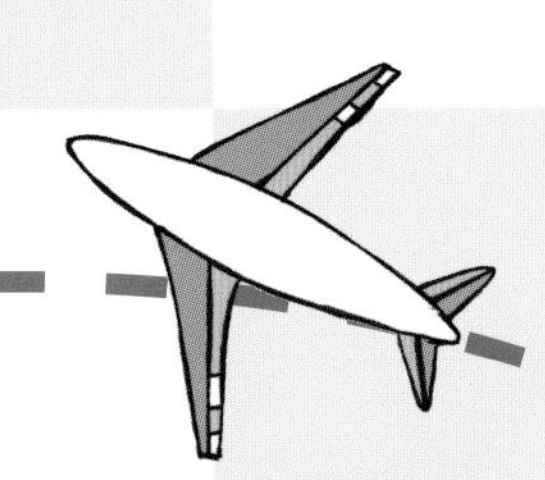

ODDS AND EVENS

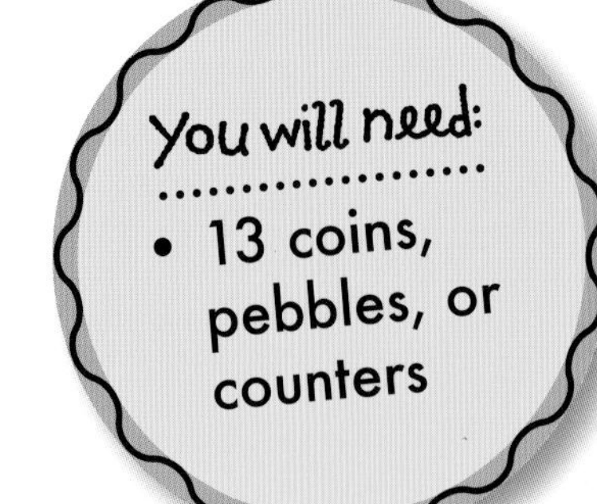

Feeling smart? Then play this game,
It's one to really test your brain.

Difficulty: ☆☆☆☆☆ **Players:** 2

1 It's easy enough to play this game, but not so easy to win. Place the 13 counters between the two players. The first player picks up either one, two or three of them and keeps them.

2 The next player does the same thing.

3 Keep going this way, Each time, you decide whether to pick up one, two, or three counters. When all the counters are gone, count how many each player has altogether.

The winner is...
the person with an even number of counters!

On Your Own?

Practice this game when you're on your own so you can begin to see how the math works.